Feral Skies: Selected Poems

2008 - 2020

By

Ken Hada

Acknowledgments

The poems selected for publication in this volume are published in several preceding collections. The author expresses grateful acknowledgment to the following publishers and their titles:

The Way of the Wind: Village Books Press, 2008

Spare Parts: Mongrel Empire Press, 2010

Margaritas & Redfish: Lamar University Press, 2013

Persimmon Sunday: Vacpoetry (Purple Flag Press), 2015

Bring an Extry Mule: Vacpoetry (Purple Flag Press), 2017

Not Quite Pilgrims: Vacpoetry (Strawberry Hedgehog Press), 2019

The Way of the Wind (2nd Edition. Fine Dog Press), 2019

Sunlight & Cedar: Vacpoetry (Strawberry Hedgehog Press), 2020

Contents

A Cedar Grove

Western cedars
along a
tall-grass prairie
frame my life.

Surviving change,
a seedy
overgrown place
harbors me.

Musing in wild
transcendence,
buoyant bluebirds
sing me back.

The Smell of Rain

I smell rain stirring
in humid air,
dusty pollen
carried on wind,
life and death mingled.

I smell rain taking me back
to childhood,
standing on a hill
overlooking a valley,
I would sniff moist air
and ride breezes
across the expanse
over a creek-bottom.

Hawks and vultures soaring
on updrafts
envied me,
envied my freedom,
my escape,
even as they would rise
and fall
and rise again
hundreds of feet at a time
without flapping a single wing.

Summer Squall

Standing on a sandy rise,
endless prairie dark at her back,
bluestem bows like paupers
before a terrible Lord.

Unflinching, she scans
charcoal skies billowing,
scarred hands finger coarse denim.

Her back straightens,
a faded red flannel shirttail flapping,
chestnut hair swirling
at the mercy of wind.

Forbidden

Beside moss-covered rocks
pushing up through a bed
of decaying oak leaves
and acorns shrouded
in effluent humus,
where a pair of cardinals
flurry through irregular limbs,
disrupts a creek trickling
into obscurity,
we lay under silent
  – and twisted cedars.

And If He Is Lucky

The first time a boy rides
his new bike, both good and bad
angels step aside to watch
the young god on two wheels
feel what can only be felt
one time in one life – breath
of heaven in his face, outpacing
the dust that claims him.

Let him fly to realms ineffable.
Soon enough, the rust of life takes
its toll. He will be grounded
in expectation, forging rivers of loss.
Let him, one time, know elation
he cannot name, a dispensation
beyond. And if he is lucky,
at least a memory will remain.

Dad's Sled

He built it with used two by fours,
scrap metal for runners.
He always saved spare parts

and cast-off material.
We might use that someday
he would say – and sure enough,

one day when ice and snow came,
the Old Bailey Hill beckoned.
I stood beside him

in the cold basement as he framed
a sled from a design
tucked away in his memory.

I helped by holding the wood
in place as he nailed it tight,
then tacked on the runners.

We rode that sled every day
the cold lasted, screaming in delight
flying downhill in home-made ecstasy.

But today I remember the making
of the sled. It is in building
that his genius lay, and how I marvel

at his ability to make happiness
out of things left over, used
and otherwise abandoned.

Little Boy Shucking Corn

A little boy shucking corn
by the burn pile out back of a broken house
stands knee-deep in silken husks.
Stalks fly in evening breeze
as he cleans yellow ears as long as his arm.
His spotted puppy sits atop his metronomic tail
fixated on the silent harvest.

A dad glances through the kitchen glass
to check on the progress of his boy.
August crickets sound and evening doves coo.
A meadowlark sits on a fence post.
Somewhere in approaching darkness,
a quail calls her covey.

Unaware of falling sky about them,
the boy concentrates on the tassels
to make ready the evening meal.
The dad knows his days are not long.
Their time will end.
This place will be abandoned.
This evening will only be memory.

He knows strand by strand
his boy is becoming a man,
but tonight, he is just thankful for the corn.

Empty Barrel

When I was a boy
I played with a blue
fifty-gallon barrel.

I passed time
making up games
drumming, listening
rolling downhill.

I remember hollow
thumping most,
gonging sounds
rising from emptiness
speaking to me.

It still does.

Fallen Limbs

I thank the ice for breaking
these limbs, dropping
them from the family tree.

I bend, pick up fallen limbs
a handful at a time, feel
bark in my fingers, sunny

wind on my neck, red
mud sticking to my boots.
I carry brokenness

uphill, aware of my steps
to a severed, scattered pile
waiting to be burned.

Today, bearing the broken
is enough – the bending,
the lifting, the touching …

Like Hawks Above Sage

Something about a prairie
makes you want to follow
flying low like hawks above sage
scattered stalks of bluestem
renegade in late October
too stubborn to die easy
too tough to be anything else.

The wind has ended. Calm
covers like glass, the world
a museum. I would pay
twice to soar once again;
I would pay double to see
from a hawk's eye cruising,
regal, sovereign, fearless.

Cimarron

A wildness that will not fade
calls in the crimson twilight.

Our tangled roots of dirt and desire and denial
are embedded in cyclical rhythms
linked to the full moon shining
over Cherokee County, pulling
the Cimarron River along
to the Arkansas, filtering sand from clay,
leaving the heron a feast,
the mallard a respite.

Survivors know these rhythms –
these voices calling out in wild red darkness.

Sliver of Moon

I saw a sliver of moon
surrounded by dark
and I felt
an uneasy comfort –
the way you feel
after winning an argument
only to isolate yourself
from the losers,
only to find yourself
on a sandy island
with nothing
but an empty sea
lashing at your feet,
nothing but the brow-beaten moon,
slim above,
dropped in heavy sky
so far away,
so far away
from anything like light.

In Darkness

In darkness
I listen to blues on the radio:
Mississippi John Hurt: *make me*
a pallet on your floor …

Lightning flashes outside, thunder
a short distance away.

Some darkness
is friendly, like a cup of tea.

You learn something
in the dark

       fringes of light.

You write down some words
you hope they like to hear
in New York

       in New York
where darkness never comes
and thunder lingers
like a dream.

Into Autumn

I plunge forward
though I often feel
I am falling
into the whirlpool
of Time.

Despite my clumsy entrance,
specks of color
pass me by.
I catch glimpses of beauty –
a sweet charade of death,
sure, one day to arrive.

Autumn is a gift
if I am secure enough
to receive it, gracious
enough to realize
what dying leaves offer,
what shadows have to say.

I am close to sixty –
a decade once remote
as stars – is now just a trail
through an oak forest
tangled with cedar and briars.

There is no turning back.

The only choice is to accept
wind in rusty leaves
for my song,
dirt beneath my feet
as a brother.

First Frost

We knew it would come.
The hay meadow
beneath pecan and elm
lies bare before an unseen
force falling.

Everything bristles.
The world is scarred,
brittle, changed –
under thin pale skin,
a heart hard as stone.

The moon is high
in empyreal sky, the sun
lags behind a hill – death's
chill arrives – seems
like only crows survive.

Frosty Morning

The frosty morning
   sits soundless
   as a saint
   in a hard pew

waiting
   to see light

   to hear
   what she already knew

before she wrapped herself
in a peasant-made shawl

   walked a few desolate blocks
   to find the place
   where she might meet her God.

In breathless silence
   dark limbs are suspended –
   there is no green
   (nothing green can stay).

   Pecan and dull cedar loom
   like murals
   on the face of the Earth.

Without sun
    there is no shadow;
Without shadows,
    we are never whole.

Winter

Days are shorter
than I want.

My cousin Bear
told me to prepare

but I was fooled
by crows at dawn

who come and go
as they please.

I am a building
a nest in the dark.

Another Intimacy

The tree frogs are so loud
tonight, we have to raise our voices
just to be heard.

Stars overwhelm black
sky – a gift
of absolute trust.

Falling fire answers
the ultimate
question – YES!

When you are so long alone,
you find another intimacy,
feel within you nothing

less – loss compensated
in countless ways –
too inscrutable to miss.

Blue River

She calls me to secluded pools
along quiet shores
beneath canopies of White Oak
and Red Cedar.

My pace slows –
thoughts diminish,
sounds hush
in this cloistered place.

I sit in shadows smoking
a soft cigar,
the full moon peaking
above the ridge.

Beyond the dense timber,
purling water
and tree frogs abide
a humble campfire.

I have no need tonight
for noise,
no desire
for that other life.

Only primal sounds matter,
these ancient rituals
merging fire and water,
earth and sky.

Water Splashing on Granite

Sometimes beauty cuts so deep
you can see clear through
to what is not there.

In this absence I see myself
most clearly, and know you
for what you are not.

We receive the sublime sometimes
unwittingly, but when the human
part glimpses that which was
and that which is to come
in a moment
we know
the curse of attraction
and the blessing of the ordinary.

Water splashing
on granite cuts a bank all the way
to the ocean and back

and like a fool I curse the rain.

Mud Turtle

Sloshing through grassy sandstone
along a lake shore I pause,
look through turbid drizzle
sense I belong beyond knowing,
breathe slow, exhaling
until I am still enough to hear
whispers of uncertain wind.

He rises out of murky water
thinking he is alone before
noticing me and disappearing
as quickly as he appeared,
dissipating ripples
the only evidence of his presence
that we in fact saw each other.

Water covers his re-entry and I
think maybe I should envy turtles,
their ability to rise and fall
unnoticed, belonging to places
where humans are merely visitors
to be reminded of unions
visceral and misunderstood.

A Short Poem

I wish I could write
a short poem everyone
would remember.

I might say: *Blessed*
are the merciful
for they shall obtain mercy

but that is already too long,
too literal –
words floating in air

without image,
needing a body, a life
to incorporate.

Old Buddha pointed
to a flower
but how can flowers bloom

when the soil
is choking on words
we refuse to hear?

Old Men

I make it a point now
to wave to old men I pass,
old men standing in shade
of a yard, maybe
a daughter's place
where now he's just a tenant
trying to understand role reversal.

I raise my forefinger
as I steer country roads or pass
through tired neighborhoods.
Most return a wave or nod *Howdy.*
Driving gives you some perspective,
shows how you might end up.

We allow something
now, especially those of us sitting
on porch swings, those
who never got around to going
somewhere, those
who still feel like something
somehow is missing.

The Weight of Your Loss

Something cruel
in not saying goodbye …

    fog on mountains, drizzle
on windshield, a buzzard
between peaks covered dark,
but beautiful from this distance,
floats invisible current, a secret
passage as close as imagination
above leafless timber dripping
gray …

    just about everyone deserves
"Goodbye" eye to eye – a mirror
for the sake of conscience …

    don't ambush me by stealing
away in the dark leaving me to carry
the weight of your loss …

Where Winter Has Been

In a green field of new clover,
eternal in its infancy,
purple and white crocus point upward
to a bluebird sky, tiny, fragile
yet strong for their effort

rising among dead brown briars,
muted cedar and twisted scrub oak,
broken limbs fallen from cottonwoods
scattered across an emerging world
where winter has been.

With the Owls

I sit quietly with the owls.
Every evening they call darkness
as sure as cloudy skies
closer than stars.

They know what they're doing.
I envy their constancy,
their sheer belief
in the way things ought to be.

Sometimes their calls
are soft, subtle,
sometimes not –
but always abrupt,

always bringing me back
to sanity, to routine,
to the goodness
God built into them.

The owls, the trees,
the darkness – this
is what matters.
This is where truth begins.

Canadian River: Purple Dawn

The bridgework at Asher nears
completion but water below,
coursing sand, needs no upgrade.

The timeless stream tugs
at me every morning I cross.
Nothing changes but light and my

limited ability to see. I see no tracks
in sand, no coyote creeping
the shores, no swallows darting

no hawks circling the somber sunless
sky, no cranes sticking upright
in shallows, no mallards clustered

in the river's turn. But I hear
the music of what I cannot see –
the river in motion is cleaner

than strings on a Martin guitar,
brighter than any score
composed by Bartok or Brahms.

River Song

Motion helps us
understand –
helps us cope.

It is right to move
downstream
to avoid stasis

to resist delusions
of permanence,
the futility

of holding on.
To feel the flowing
around me,

through me
is life.
To be one

with the current –
this much
is real.

Like A Fenceless Sky

I wish for the days of coyote-filled nights
when stars were known and you could hear
slow-rising vapor from frosty hollows
or berries on cedar popping to life.

I long to be held like a sleeping child
with tomorrow's dream tucked in a blanket
where loneliness ends like a fenceless sky.

I want to build where nomads are free
to roam and war is no longer fought
for oil, or water, where howling with time,
is commonplace, the careful stirring
of coffee at daybreak and yesterday's moon.

When I Dream

the branches quicken
green, snow melts, grass
emerges overnight …

when I dream

policeman don't shoot
us and preachers remain true
to their first love …

when I dream

color unites us, warms
our cold hands by a fire
glowing small and still

branches quicken
green, snow melts, grass
flourishes in dark night

when I dream.

Security Guard

His skin was perceived
to be too dark.
Guarding the Holocaust Museum

was another flaw.
Preserving a shrine to events
that never happened

threatens white lies.
A pale terrorist rifled
his prey to expunge

delusions of common humanity.
Taking a bullet
for us all proves not only

that the Holocaust occurred,
but for some
it never ended.

What Gandhi And Christ Have Over Me

I am not
the change
I want.

I am a crow
picking
at roadkill.

All my acumen
flutters
in darkness.

The Anchor

Look inward, there is a field
inside you full of daisies
and clover, honeybees
and all the things to make a soul.

All around you is dying gas –
a suffocating mirror,
an unfulfilled guest,
frustrated lust

but deep within the field
at sunrise, or in midnight
the breeze stirs, pollen floats
and you know there is more

to life than cubicles and charts,
keyboards and media bombs.
You know the anchor is rusting;
soon you will break free.

Prayer

Some weeks ago, I buried bulbs
in the yard. With a shovel
I dug around the pecan tree,
and on my knees, placed bulbs
into ground, then by hand
returned the soil, patting it
into place to cover the wounds
I caused. I rose, and for good
measure, tamped the dirt
firm with the soul of my boot –
a righteous feeling – my feet
entreating timeless earth –
what good we do follows
the good we believe.

Crepe Myrtle

The foreign bush I planted
flowers again, despite
heat and lack of rain.

Common in Oklahoma,
so common everywhere,
we forget its origin.

Brilliant color flaming
in my prairie yard
will not permit me
to surrender idealism,
as if anyone owns beauty.

A Chestnut Mare

bends her head
over barbed wire.

Yellow tail swishes
supple skin. Hard

flesh glimmers.
Sage surrounds her.

A windmill turns
in the distance.

Pelicans on Lake Keystone

They arrived in the night
ahead of the lightning storm.
Broad wings deflecting
nervous wind, they took refuge
in a cove, huddled in darkness.

This morning, in bright sun
they bounce on brown water
dipping curious orange bills
into choppy currents.

A few rise in flight above the old
Arkansas riverbed – taut wings
bend, circle in perfect loops
in clean October sky.

I look up, follow their flight.
I look into their eyes:
I swear, they are smiling.

When I Was A Heron

I stalked the slippery shallows
as quiet as a falling star.
I hated the motorized boats
crisscrossing the rocky currents.
I did my fishing close to shore
near those dead overhanging logs.
I waited with a perfect eye,
and with precise timing I speared
the fish, graciously unaware.

It was those days when I was young
when the stars did not disappear
though the barn light burned and kitchen
candles flickered until pink dawn.
There was plenty; there was restraint.
It was then you heard me squawking
as the sun dropped into gray hills
and I knew darkness, like all things
good, was nothing to keep.

Sand Plums on The Canadian River

He walks the lesser part of day
along the river's path slipping
through shifting sand, eyes
pierced for plumpest, ripest

picks. His face is course, his
fingers hard, he squints away
the western sun – a pail of plums
half full, meadowlarks in flight.

Cathedral in the Grass

She sits cross-legged
under yellow grass that stands
belly-high to a horse
in a field far enough away
where a parent could not hear giggles,
could not see him crouched
on nine-year-old knees
looking reverently
at her shining auburn hair.

Afternoon shadows lengthen
across her, wrap around
to her pink mouth and hazel eyes
gleaming at his squeamishness
while keeping watch
on their favorite place to hide.

Looking back, he hopes only
to be forgiven
for *not* worshiping.

Hunger

One night I built a fire
in my backyard.

I got so lonely
I went in the house,
got two ears of corn,
wrapped them in foil,
placed them in the fire

then tonged them out,
half-hot, unwrapped them
in darkness and ate
kernel by kernel
as if we were best friends,
melted butter dripping
out of my mouth.

Isn't it something
what hunger will do?

Compensation

I come here because I want to hear rain
dripping through pines when no one else
is around, to feel December wind
wrap around me while I gather twigs,
damp and soggy needles to kindle fire
to thaw my bones enclosed, withdrawn
like pine cones in the lonely chill.

Smoke brims my eyes, tickles my lungs
while chartreuse flames lick oblate cones
as compensation for solitude.

I hear new silence hovering in the pines,
the steady, unhurried rain patting
the roof, an occasional flame popping
in the remaining coals.

Skeleton

A wounded doe limps
in shadows of evening sun.
I watch her struggle, watch
her looking for something
over her shoulder.

She circles, then settles
in shallow grass – her
dark eyes transfixed.

By morning, she is gone.
I walk the field, stumble
to the fence.

I find a fawn's skeleton,
remains of the ravaged –
a tiny pile of bones
picked clean – glistening
white in morning sun.

A Herd of Antelope, Extraordinarily Beautiful

after Chekhov, Ward No. 6

When the prayers have ended
other are just begun.

The days inside
and the time outside
may really be the same

but where then is the source of dreams?
What do the dying see
that the living overlook?

Except for beauty too little
considered and grace, rarely perceived

dying is to be alive
even as living is dying.

On New Mexico's table land
I have seen a herd of antelope,
extraordinarily beautiful
and graceful
                    the sun
in the morning glimmers,
silver singing between us.

I sigh,

sigh for them, for us all.

As you pray, remember,
even God runs with the herd.

Yellow Cottonwoods

There's heartache in these lines
cracking through once-hard
ground crumbling to dust.

Sadness drifts here
under yellow cottonwoods
where old men sit
in a distorted circle – a parlor
for the ornery and rejected
where a can of beer
accompanies a worn story
told with fading bravado
swallowing fear in quick gulps.

These grains of river sand
drying in wind sift
through time, pile around toes
of shuffling boots, legs
dangling off a tailgate
or sitting awry in a chair
whose fabric is stretched
past the point of brittle.

Chicory in the Ditches

When first light calms blue-swept night
and cool dawn erases
yesterday's heat.

Morning reminds us that night
is a fragment, and summer
swelter is brief.

Blue flowers color the day
in dew-filled grass. We find
ourselves in song.

We are made for the morning.
Starting over is something
we should get right.

Blue

for Tim Tingle

A rainy blue night
the car wheels sound
oddly soothing, jazz
horn sweeping low

I drive through heavy sky
as if on the other side
someone knows me,
as if morning will call

my name. At the gate
I pause, feel the steel
chain in my palm, turn
the key – empty trees,

dead grass, always.
Somewhere, someone
on a small boat at sea
stands on deck, sniffs

silent air, as I do now.
My lungs fill with cedar
and humidity. I think
about many things.

A Night Like This

The earth seems to stand still.
Coyotes bark, a neighbor's dog
and stars above – what stars
we have, we have – and I
want them all. On nights
like this, blue stem, belly high
in the field, is silent, no wind
every slight sound is heard:
a fish splash at the pond edge
a screen door squeaks.

I want the stars, the post oaks
tall and serene, I want it all,
want to know it all, be it all.
Fallen leaves crackle
beneath my boots. My dog
walks a little quieter, more light
on his feet. He hears the coyotes
too – we both stop to listen
and I think we both know
what we are listening for.

My breath plumes, mixes
with cigar smoke. I lean
against an oak – on a night
like this I want to forgive
so many things – if I could
just find the right star.

Timberline

I've come to these mountains
to grieve, to breathe,
fade above timberline,
high above domestic claims.

Up here rocks burnished
by wind, melting snow
and unfiltered sun, color
the lake before me.

Up here lightning strikes
from glaucous clouds
stalk the vastness,
pierce even hardest peaks.

I consider my next move,
realize I could wait too long
(but unsure when that would be),
not wanting to miss the splendid event.

Tonight, I will sleep below alpine
flowers in a grove of birch.
Hear night settle, indulge
in simple breath.

Stars

for Debbie

Everything we know
is in the past, stars
burning out above

us, twittering spots
of light fall through time
making the darkness

livable. Better
to know old ways, the
former loves, other

lives in retrospect.
Then again, how could
one know anything

before it fell, white
gas filling space, the
void of a moment?

Heat Lightning

flashes through trembling sky
crossing horizons
I must never outgrow.

Feeble clouds mark
its path. Heaven's fire
skirts the rim of earth.

From this sandy knoll
I watch with wonder,
glowing like a newborn.

Wind

On a January morning
when the sun seems new,
frost-covered cedars
dance like lovers
in private bliss.

The Apostle John wrote
about wind – an unseen,
undeniable force. Others
did as well – Rumi, Hafiz,
Khayyam and Gibran.

I take comfort knowing
Jesus isn't the only voice
crying in vacant places
at vacuous times – intervals
of history – when a friend

may be nebulous, ethereal.
Truth is not something shouted
or pursued with a sword.
Crusades – though prevalent –
still fight the wind.

Wind Song

Tell me secrets
in the night-sky;
whisper lines
the ancients knew.

Night voices sing
hope, fire
imagination,
kindle souls

into red-flame
that destroys
but purges,
re-seeds,

creating –
these Saturnian voices
singing
of transience.

Dogwood

Brief flowers
teach me
your mountain secrets:

To flourish
in harshness,
to flower
in shadows.

Dark Comes to Caney Hollow

The last birdsong.

Hardly a sound
above a tiny creek.

Barely a breeze.

Soon there will be no sun.

Through distant limbs
dim amber light
inside a cabin

seems all the more remarkable
for its persistence.

Feeding Sheep

for Beci

They hear her stepping
through grass and stone.
They know her gait,
tremble with anticipation
beside empty troughs.

She talks to them
like a child –
her hand reaching
through wire, offering
the first taste of morning.

In these electric moments
life begins again –
raspy tongue, wet nose
touching the flesh
of palms upturned.

Two Horses in Morning Red

Their backs glow
as if April sun
itself.

They must feel
the warmth, steam
escaping

their nostrils,
wet flanks
in dewy grass.

Do they know
how beautiful
they are

standing alone
like angels
on a nameless hill

radiating
Eternity's fire?
Do they know

how I need
to be consumed
with their flame?

Thunder in the Morning

Of all the sounds that frame my hearing
nothing stirs me like thunder in the morning,
sends me to a preternatural state of hope,
compensates in ways I don't expect,
a gift from a cosmos I can only imagine.

I remember lilies around the walnut tree
the last thing I saw before sleep.
I hear birds singing through raindrops,
the swoop of wind through April leaves.

The world I manage is often parched,
athirst with wrongheaded desire,
dusty souls in need of a good stirring.

Often

Often, I open the door to let in
the sound of rain tapping
along with a Brahms symphony
or the Allman Brothers – often
my pen cannot keep pace
with the dropping water
or the chilling violins or
the tragic guitars – often
I remind myself that rain,
like music, like a pen moving
on paper, is what the world
needs most. It could be
that the thunder outside
is no match for the singing birds
at rainy dawn. It could be
that the collection of their voices
is a light that brings us home.

Warblers in May

after Myriam Fraga

Duke Ellington's swing band starts
Tuesday morning. Coffee and chicory,
New Orleans style, helps me find

the back stoop. I unlock the door, step
into timeless sage and hardwoods.

Hear the warblers. Stop. Listen close.
Marvelous trilling every horn player mimics.

Sit with me, won't you? Sit with me
in the first streaks of light. Let's sit
a good long while, what's the hurry?

Everything moves too fast. We've hijacked
ourselves, hostage to ransom we cannot pay.

Our boat tumbles in the waves. Clinging
to a capsizing boat, we survive because we are lucky.
In the waves we promise to be better …

Sit with me a while.
Sit and listen
to the warblers in May.

9 788182 538573